Poetic Justice

Legal Humor In Verse

JD DuPuy
ML Philpott

Copyright © 2013 Poetic Justice, LLC
All rights reserved.

ISBN: 0-9891401-0-5
ISBN-13: 978-0-9891401-0-2

ISBN: 0-9891401-1-3 (ebook)
ISBN-13: 978-0-9891401-1-9 (ebook)

For everyone who persists in the practice of law.

Contents

Tales From the Table

Life in the Firm

Disillusionment: The Limericks

Introduction

This is not a book of lawyer jokes.

If you're wondering the punchline to, "What's the difference between a lawyer and a catfish?" you won't find it here. We're not laughing at lawyers. We're laughing *with* lawyers. Well, we're kind of laughing at lawyers – but in the sense that lawyers can laugh at themselves.

This book is *for* lawyers. Also for law students, former lawyers, and the non-lawyers who work and live with lawyers. It's for everyone who's in on the joke: Everyone who has witnessed the eccentric personalities and bizarre situations particular to this field of work. Everyone who, even just for a second, has wondered if they should have gone to medical school, culinary school... anything other than law school. Everyone who has ever looked around at the characters and events of their day and thought, "No one would even believe me if I told them about this."

We believe you.

Opening Statement

Well, some say we're a homogenous group,
That we make the exact same impression,
And others crack wise on continuous loop
Making fun of our chosen profession.

We beg to differ and hope you will agree
That the law is full of varied characters.
Just because each attorney has a J.D.
Doesn't mean we're alike to the letter.

It's true – there are types, in real life as in art,
And you'll find several in these pages
Ranging from classmates to judges to partners
From everybody's law career stages.

The fact is, we're unique *and* we're similar:
As much as each lawyer is different,
We share something, no matter where we are –
Big firm or small, in-house, or government.

So if humor gets you through the day, read on,
And gather 'round, ye Latin-speaking nerds,
Let down your guard, relax, and get your laugh on,
You may find yourself somewhere in these words.

Law School

It's not quite the best of times (maybe the worst?)
Just wait – this three-year-long bubble will burst

Time Warp

Gossip, insecurity, competition, cliques…
Wasn't it a decade ago we outgrew all this?

Sorting out the pecking order like teenagers do,
Obsessed with rank, we watch our backs and watch each other, too.

We've got all kinds of females here, from prom queens to wallflowers,
Mean girls, dull ones, sporty types, and ones who don't take showers.

The guys are represented too, from quarterbacks to nerds,
Jerkwads, class clowns, and the ones in love with their own words.

The romances are epic, and the breakups make the news,
There's not a social situation we don't see as win or lose.

Professors play supporting roles, engrossed in their subjects,
We ridicule them, roll our eyes, "lol" at them by text.

Ambitions worn on every sleeve, there's much pontification.
We're always preening for an audience, giving an oration.

Why did I think there would be no nonsense of this kind?
Clearly there's a lot we grownup kids can't leave behind.

They say, "Look left and then look right. One of you won't make it."
I think I may nominate myself. I'm not sure I can take it.

Blackacre

With apologies to TS Eliot

August is the cruelest month, actually,
As fresh faces peel open hornbooks
To master the ins and outs of all
Manner of perturbation
Committed, implausibly, in the same hypothetical place,
The setting for each case:
Blackacre.

How would it feel
To be a resident of this doomed habitat,
Each tranquil summer brought to an end
With a new litter of law babies
And their grizzled professors feeding them lessons
On the confusion, loopholes, stupidity, and greed
That never fail to arise?

It starts in autumn, this backyard chaos:
A conveys his tract to B for life,
Subject to some shifting executory interest
That never seems to pan out.
C accidently becomes landlocked
Because of his ridiculous lack of foresight.
D, forgetting that future generations always disappoint,
Foolishly plans for his children's children's children to own a piece.
Will they, the ungrateful urchins?
We can only wait-and-see.

Over time, things turn uglier.
C quietly erects a fence in a remote corner
Of A's land. Plotting. Planning. Possessing.
T starts walking about, in places he should not be,
Throwing his cigarette butts into barrels
Of unidentifiable liquid that may or may not be flammable.
There is not a nuisance in all the land
That won't be discovered by a small child's hand.
The swimming pool, it seems, was constructed on top
Of an abandoned mine, which happens to be full of fireworks.
This would pose quite a threat to the family of
Domesticated ostriches that live on the land,
But for the fact that most of them are dead already,
Victims of inadvertent poisoning by insecticide applied wrong.
Careful, child!

Winter brings no end to trouble.
L swore that he knew nothing of the chimpanzee
Locked in the basement of the home rented to T,
Or at least he did not know it was dangerous.
He went next door to A's house, a place
He had been many times before, to talk about
His troubling situation with T.
But there he was greeted by a spring-gun.
(Everyone on Blackacre seems to own one.)

And then, just like that, it's over.
Well read and well versed, they move on.
And shell-shocked, the characters are once again at rest,
Thankful at least not to live on Whiteacre.
(You should see the shit that happens there.)

Hey Gunner, Gunner

Hey gunner, gunner,
Like a marathon runner,
From the starting line, you're setting the pace.
Sucking up to the professor,
Knocking down those who are lesser,
Even Socrates can't beat you in this race.

Hey gunner, gunner,
You're a bit of a bummer,
The vexing bane of every study group.
While your notes may be far better,
Perfect right down to the letter,
You are grating on the nerves of the whole troop.

Hey gunner, gunner,
Your resume's a stunner,
And you ace every single interview.
When you apply for every spot,
The chances basically are shot,
For those who aren't the editor of Law Review.

Hey gunner, gunner,
Have you not stopped to wonder,
About this contest you have bought into?
When midnight oil is burning bright
And you're up working half the night
Will it still feel like a victory to you?

Grades Were Supposed to Be Posted Online
An Hour Ago – A Haiku

Click Click Click Click Click
Click Click Click Click Click Click Click
Click Click Click Click Click

Write On

You might think it would be time for me to relax,
As spring exams were finally through,
Yet though I was weary, I still made the choice:
I'd attempt to write on Law Review.

I'd have 5 days to summon one last blast of genius
(as if I'd had any to start with),
To sort through a mountain of sources and cases,
And whip up 30 pages of pith.

If it worked, I'd end up with my name in print,
And my job prospects likely would spike,
But to jump into writing right after exams?
Let me try to explain what that's like:

Like swimming the English Channel against the tide, then
Digging straight down to the Chunnel;
Or milking a hundred cantankerous cows, then
Drinking it all through a funnel.

Like running a marathon through the dark woods, then
Sewing a blanket from spider webs;
Or building a house with a hammer and saw, then
Assembling a row of kids' bunk beds.

Like loading a whole moving truck single-handed, then
Making a paper-mâché bookshelf.
Or driving cross-country without any sleep, then
Changing your tires by yourself.

Like going on Celine Dion's worldwide tour, then
Transcribing *Titanic*, each word;
Or birthing triplets after two days of labor, then
Dancing *Swan Lake* as the bird.

Like licking the floor of an entire mall clean, then
Snorkling for pennies in the fountain;
Or going 10 times on the Crazy Teacups, then
Doing back handsprings to Splash Mountain.

So you see how it went – I'm ashamed to admit
That I gave up, my brain was all gone,
But not before indulging one last delusion:
The thought that I might just grade on.

The Idealist

Everyone knew her in law school,
With her sandals and that long braid of hair,
So intent on "making a difference,"
Righting wrongs and making life fair.

We ought not to have underestimated her,
For while she ranted on the clubbing of seals,
She studied hard and showed all the prepsters
The summer associate spots she could steal.

She picked a gig at a big DC firm,
Where she'd have the government's ear,
Funny, she seemed a bit muted
Upon her return for second year.

By her last semester, she had traded
Most of her lofty concerns
For new notions about tax code loopholes,
Having learned what a lobbyist earns.

Last I heard, she was caught in a hotel
With a senator, striking a deal,
On behalf of an oil company whose last spill
Killed hundreds of thousands of seals.

A Very Short List

At a loss for what to do with my Bachelor of Arts
I figured law school was as good a use as any for my smarts.

Not that I loved the thought of my whole life as an attorney,
But at least I'd have three years to figure out my career journey.

People said, "Why, you can do so much if you earn a J.D.!"
So I buckled down, invested my hard work, time, and money.

Now here I am, ready to find that perfect opportunity,
I've made a list of all the options, things I'm now prepared to be:

A lawyer.

Bar Exam:
A Mental Conversation with Fate
(For the Terrified)

And now, the greatest test of all,
The big event – no time to stall,
My future lies in one exam,
OH GOD, I need more time to cram.

> *Inhale. Exhale. One breath at a time.*
> *You've studied hard – you'll be just fine.*

My heart is beating in my ears,
I'm going to need a new career,
There's no way I've done enough.
It's not my fault! There's just so much!

> *You know it all, inside and out,*
> *It's go-time now, forget your doubt.*

Multistate. Essays. Woe unto me.
(At least I passed the MPRE.)
Fear hits me like a tsunami.
I'm blacking out! I want my mommy!

> *Go ahead and hit the floor.*
> *When you come to, here's what's in store:*
> *Somehow you'll pass (your score will do),*
> *Like plenty of morons who came before you.*

Bar Exam:
A Mental Conversation with Fate
(For the Confident)

[Yawn] I'm so ready for this test.
Why is everyone so stressed?
I skipped most test prep classes,
(Though I'm sure they helped the masses.)

> *Careful! Ego could be your downfall,*
> *Don't blow it off and botch it all –*

There's just no need to fuss and worry,
Study too much and things get blurry.
I learned it all during law school,
The thing to do is play it cool.

> *Oh, boy – it looks like it's too late.*
> *That attitude will seal your fate.*

I've already lined up a sweet job,
A step ahead of most of these slobs.
What time is it? How long will it be
Until I'm done with this formality?

> *Looking ahead – a classic mistake,*
> *This is going to end in heartache.*
> *When reality hits perhaps you'll see:*
> *You've always got February.*

Big Firm, Small Firm

And now a pair of poems in the style of Dr. Seuss,
who was even better at nonsense words than lawyers

One fish, two fish.
Me fish, you fish.

Which is it I'd rather be?
A big fish in a little sea?
Or small fish in the big city?

This one has a little town.
That one has a golden crown.

Should it be the sweet slow pace?
Or shiny high rise, fast rat race?

Two offers, no time left to stall.
Let's have it out, Big v. Small.

* * *

Small Town: Your daily greeting – smiling faces.
Big City: You'll get to work on landmark cases.

Small Town: The action's slow, but you're the man.
Big City: Big money – wasn't that the plan?

Small Town: A four-man firm, you're part of things!
Big City: Hot paralegals, office flings.

Small Town: Here they're friendly, there they're mean.
Big City: (Enjoy date night at Dairy Queen.)

Small Town: There's time to spare, relax and laugh.
Big City: It's such fun screaming at the staff.

Small Town: Think how close to Mom you'll be!
Big City: (Small Town, dumbass, that's a point for me.)

Small Town: You'll get to see your kids and spouse.
Big City: How 'bout a new vacation house?

Small Town: It's yours when senior guy retires.
Big City: You'll reap the perks of frequent fliers.

Small Town: You might die bored, but here you're safe.
Big City: The cash is great, the hours chafe.

(Perhaps the problem isn't *where*,
But *what* I'm doing, here or there.)

The Decision: Litigation v. Transactional

Seuss, take two

One fish, two fish.
Me fish, you fish.

Which will be my life's vocation?
Will I go with litigation?
Or transactional negotiation?

Eventually, I have to pick,
And must attempt to make it stick.

Indecision and unrest…
How to choose what suits me best?

Two options. Please let's shed some light,
Compare them both: Deal v. Fight

* * *

Transactional: There's power in making sure others comply.
Litigation: The feel of that first courtroom win is a high.

Transactional: Put things together (though they may lack in glamour).
Litigation: When things fall apart, keep 'em outta the slammer!

Transactional: Are you up for a lifetime of Commercial Code?
Litigation: When you lose in court, will your self-worth erode?

Transactional: Drafting a proxy statement's boring as hell.
Litigation: Honestly, most cases don't go to trial.

Transactional: Like reading fine print? You'll do that a lot.
Litigation: It's just like *Law & Order* on TV. (Not.)

Transactional: Long office hours, handcuffed to your chair.
Litigation: You're a slave to each case, schedule up in the air.

Transactional: Ace all the details and crush… punctuation.
Litigation: Travel in style, but miss family vacation.

Transactional: It's all fun and games 'til you hit a recession.
Litigation: The work never slows; nor does your depression.

Transactional: I've perfected maneuvers like "cut" and "paste."
Litigation: I tell myself this hasn't been a big waste.

(It hits me now: The zero-sum game.
This or *that*, the end's the same.)

Logic Question for the Regretful

To succeed at legal analysis
You must prove that you possess
The skill to pick apart a knot
To find the clues others cannot.

For instance: "A liberal arts grad
Without support from mom or dad
Or any sort of professional clue
Or better ideas for what to do

Enrolls in a three-year program
Without giving even half a damn
For exactly what the outcome will be
When he or she obtains that degree

And then the student graduates
And comes to realize much too late
This is not the person he or she
Ever really wanted to be."

Which of the following arguments
Would seem to make the greatest sense?

A) A time machine could fix it all.
B) That mountain of debt will one day be small.
C) "You'll grow to love it, wait and see."
D) You can't undo a law degree.

Brand New Attorney

Making cash and decisions, finally free,
While the ink's still drying on that new degree

A Few Haiku

Measuring Time

Remember sun, moon,
day, night, week, year? Now it's all
six-minute increments.

Employment Rates

Well-meaning friends ask,
"What type law will you practice?"
Any type that hires.

Lady Lawyer Dress Code

I.
Skirts must graze the knee.
Suits in conservative shades.
Librarian hair.

II.
Casual Friday:
Cardigans with tasteful slacks.
Now we're letting loose.

The Lawyer's Spouse

That won't work on me;
I'm not opposing counsel.
"Objection," my ass.

Cease and Desist

50 paragraphs,
300 commas, therefores,
Just to say: Stop it.

Inspiration

I'm just positive
Thurgood Marshall got his start
Doing doc review.

Conference Call

"This guy's a dumbass,"
I said after hitting mute.
Oops. Didn't hit mute.

Personal Injury Lawyer

An ambulance wails.
"Shouldn't you be chasing that?"
My friends are assholes.

The Call Not Taken

With a wink in Robert Frost's direction

Two lines diverged on a Mylar plat,
And to one call I could not commit,
And being new here, sweating I sat,
And wondered just how it could be that
A single line could seemingly split.

One line was an easement of some sort,
But which was which? I was doomed to fail.
The clock was ticking, time had grown short,
And as my guts started to contort,
I sat alone and chewed my thumbnail.

Being young and scared, I dared not ask
My cruel senior partner for his take,
For fear of catching merciless flack,
Or being the victim of a wisecrack,
When he realized I was a fake.

So I chose the one that I thought right,
With anxiety and doubts acute.
Two lines diverged on a plat and I,
I called the one less traveled by,
And that led to my malpractice suit.

The harder the conflict, the more glorious the triumph.
- Thomas Paine

YES.

This is how victory feels.

This is how the air of success smells.

This is how a winner struts that stuff.

This is how to tell a judge what's what.

This is how a brand-new badass lawyer GETS IT DONE.

This is how to spin it later: Leave out "unopposed."

The Happy Lawyer

Sit down, young one, let me tell you the facts
'Bout the creature beloved to be real
By law students, undergrads, TV fans:
The Happy Lawyer – that mythic idea).

We've all been maintaining the illusion,
So your faith would propel your pursuit
Of this work, but it's all a delusion,
A fairy tale; now it's time for the truth.

Are those tears…? Are you…? Oh my God… crying?
Oh, how awkward, I didn't expect this.
No, of course, I was kidding – just lying,
Happy Lawyers… sure … they exist!

In fact, yes, I think I heard recently
One defended the, um… Easter Bunny.
Yes! That's right, she did it quite decently,
Took his case for not one cent of money.

There now, you see? Perhaps you've heard also
Of the time she helped out Santa Claus?
When she copyrighted, "Ho Ho Ho,"
She earned a sleigh bell for helping the cause.

Oh, and of course, there were the leprechauns.
I heard a Happy Lawyer saved their gold,
When they invested only to be conned.
(Without her, their rainbow would've been sold.)

So buck up! Dry your eyes! Believe what you must!
Unicorns, mermaids, all that magic stuff…
Happy Lawyers are everywhere – have trust!
You'll be one too, if you work hard enough.

Return to Sender

What is this guy's problem?
Why is he such an ass?
We're all on the same team here,
Man, show some freakin' class.

He sent an email to my whole team,
Blasting us all to bits.
I know the man's a big shot partner,
But he's ruthless with his hits.

Huh. My friend just wrote him back.
Told him we'll try to do better.
Pffff... I'd rather tell him where he can shove
His nasty email letter.

Here. I'll write my friend to complain
About this self-righteous douche.
"Sounds like somebody needs to get laid,"
And now to hit send: *whoosh*

Wait. Something doesn't feel quite right.
I hear whispering out in the hall.
I couldn't have?! Oh, no. I did.
Damn you, Reply All.

The Odd Couple

I wonder if we'd know each other
In another sort of circumstance?
I think if we're both being honest,
We would have to say there's not a chance.

Between your fondness for fan fiction
And my love of fantasy football,
There's no overlap in our interests.
It would seem we share nothing at all.

The spilled coffee on my desk grows mold;
You are neat to a fault, can't stand mess.
But here, side by side in the trenches,
These differences couldn't count less.

When I lose a motion in court and
Come back feeling low and downtrodden,
You nod along as I curse the world,
And I feel a little less rotten.

When up to your elbows in paper,
You know my light will be on late, too.
You're searching for some obscure detail,
And I'm digging through files, just like you.

Sometimes we like to go "out to lunch"
Scarfing sandwiches out in the hall,
Before going back to our own desks
To handle another client call.

We made up "Name That Paralegal,"
A guessing game we've been known to play,
Just to take a break from the madness
While stuck at work on a Saturday.

It works rather well we're so busy,
As what busies us bonds us as well.
In fact, you're the best part of this job
When the caseload gets crazy as hell.

We've turned into allies, compadres.
Though related by just this one thing,
We've grown up in this family of sorts,
Not work spouses – more like work siblings.

Nursery Rhymes: An Ethics Primer

Remember: You'll do fine, you can't go too wrong
(Unless you screw it up… in which case, so long)

Confidentiality

Jack and Jill went out to lunch
To talk about a case.
Jack blabbed too loud
In a close-sitting crowd
And spilled secrets all over the place.

Competency

Hey diddle diddle
You know just a little
About criminal cases of course.
But don't try to defend
Your drunk-driving friend,
If your specialty's tax or divorce.

Dipping Into Trust Accounts

A-tisket a-tasket,
Stay out of your client's basket.
You set up a trust, and guard it you must,
And never touch one nickel in it.
Don't skim it,
Don't spend it,
And for God's sake don't borrow against it,
You'll end up disbarred, you'll be feathered and tarred.
Just resist, or you'll live to regret it.

Conflict of Interest

Rub a dub dub
Take care not to make this flub:
When you pick up a lateral hire,
Keep from walking a high wire.
If he helped the other side,
Special rules must be applied.
When the lawyer is installed,
Super-size that Chinese Wall.

Billing Abuses

Hickory Dickory Dock
Beware: Don't run up the clock.
Think charging double
Won't land you in trouble?
When you're censured you're in for a shock.

Drinking on the Job

Humpty Dumpty sat at the bar.
Humpty Dumpty went five drinks too far.
All the strong coffee, and all the breath mints
Couldn't make afternoon hearings make sense.

Returning Calls

Little boy blue, get on the horn!
Your clients have left messages,
Their nerves are getting worn.
If you don't return the call
Even when the matter's small
The State Bar will hear about it.
(You can't say you've not been warned.)

Swindling the Elderly

Some like it hot,
Some like it cold,
Some take advantage of their clients
Who are weak and old.

Ethical it's not,
Don't say you haven't been told:
Don't plug your name into their wills
To inherit all their gold.

Personal Relationships

Little Miss Pliant
Slept with her client
Despite what the ethics rules say.
"Shouldn't we end it?"
Asked the defendant
When he realized he'd still have to pay.

Soliciting Clients

It's raining, it's pouring,
The rules aren't for ignoring.
If you coerce, or worse, harass,
Prospective clients who didn't ask,
You might as well be whoring.

In Court

A world like no other: It has its own rules
The language is strange, and the characters are jewels

The Raven

With a tip of the hat to Edgar Allen Poe

Once upon a morning dreary, in a courtroom, feeling weary,
I wondered which judge would emerge from behind the chamber door,
Whilst I sat reviewing notes, the deputy, he cleared his throat,
"All rise," he said. A figure appeared. Under my breath I swore,
"Not again," I muttered quietly and looked down to the floor,
'Twas the judge I most abhorred.

As his ebony wings around him flapped, he settled his robe in his lap,
Pasted slick like greasy feathers, his thin black hair he wore,
It would be enough – his dour pose, beady eyes, and beaklike nose –
To earn his nickname of "The Raven," but in fact, what he was known for,
Was the way he shot down anything you ever asked for,
His favorite phrase: "Nevermore."

Despite the arguments I made, it seemed he never could be swayed,
I would always come up short asking, "May it please the court…"
When my client broke probation (hit a cop while on vacation)
I asked the judge for grant of bail, fearing it was of no avail;
I knew what he would say before he even heard what I hoped for,
Quoth the Raven, "Nevermore."

I once took on a soft drink maker for being a trademark taker,
Seemed so obvious to me that this rule breaker was done for,
If a drink called "Mountain Spew" came in a bottle of green hue,
Would infringement seem to you like the right answer in this war?
But the judge drank nothing more, he was a Spew fan to the core,
Quoth the Raven, "Nevermore."

Had a case ripe for dismissal and let out a victory whistle
Summary judgment was in order to be sure!
Though the case was clearly flimsy, it was subject to his whimsy
And I knew as soon as I saw opposing counsel take the floor,
He'd have eyes for only her, such was her busty blonde allure,
Quoth the Raven, "Nevermore."

Then came my time to shine, and the stars they did align,
I'd defend an easy one, the anchorman from Channel 4
Who'd been caught in a misdeed (just a pocket full of weed),
Got the DA to agree he'd plea for keeping jail time short,
But His Honor's mood was poor, and he killed my chance to score,
Quoth the Raven, "Nevermore."

So, on that morning dreary, my mood… well, it was not cheery,
And when I realized it was he, what I'd be in for,
A sudden rage, it blinded me, so fed up I could hardly see.
I grabbed my overstuffed briefcase, and without the least remorse,
Chucked it across the courtroom toward the bench and to the floor,
As I screamed it: "NEVERMORE!"

Voir Dire

I scan across the crowded room
At faces glazed with sleep and gloom.
A jury summons brought them here
For the hell on earth that is voir dire.

Though I admit, I do despair
Of finding twelve who'll try to care
About my client – poor, screwed guy –
I've got to give it my best try.

I'll ask great questions, find the gold
Deep within each civilian soul.
I'll find the ones who make the grade!
(And thus begins the freak parade.)

***

Number Four hates gays.
Number Eight blames blacks.
Number Nine says he "won't pay no damn income tax."

Ten can see the dead,
Thirteen's had four lives,
Sixteen claims marriage to a batch of alien wives.

Twenty is asleep,
Twenty-two smells of beer,
Twenty-seven swears she has a crippling mustache fear.

Thirty has meth teeth,
Thirty-six owns twelve cats,
Thirty-nine is inked up with some terrifying tats.

Forty-one just screamed,
Forty-four has a flask,
Is Forty-six really wearing a Darth Vader mask?

***

No number of peremptory strikes
Could yield a crew I'm going to like.
The best advice I'll give today
Is one word to my client: Pray.

The Generalist

It was Monday morning, calendar call,
When I first heard his voice, that thick Southern drawl.
He sat in the back, so I turned to see,
In a room of dark suits, an old man in khaki.
Not a day under 80, he looked quite well,
Like a spry kind of guy with a story to tell.
I watched him that morning as he watched all of us,
Seeming vaguely amused at our young-lawyer fuss.

So I sought him out later when court was complete,
Here was a character I wanted to meet.
I told him a bit of my brief history,
And how I practiced family law, specifically,
When I asked him his specialty, he raised an eyebrow,
And what he said next I can hear even now:
"Son," he said wryly, "I'm a generalist."
I stopped cold – a what? – do they still exist?

Could the same guy who handles a custody dispute
Turn around and take on a sentence to commute,
And then later meet with an Estates clerk,
To file the Final Account paperwork?
Yes, he said, he could meet any client's need,
He'll even search titles in the Registry.
He knows landlord-tenant, wills and trusts too,
It seems there is nothing he can't or won't do.

He's practiced this way for 50-plus years,
But sadly, he said, he's the last of his peers.
Many of them had grown dissatisfied
When it became all the rage to be board certified.
"It's all so complex now," he said in frustration,
"The profession was killed by *specialization*."
The Golden Age of law, he felt, had faded,
Leaving the legends like him rather jaded.

Such a relic he was, this old-school law guy,
I hated to shake his hand and say goodbye.
Though I'd have loved to hear more of what he said,
We both had a full day of work still ahead,
I was unsure where next I'd see him, or when,
But I guessed his wide path might cross mine again.
He faded from view as he drifted away
In a crowd of not-so-special specialists that day.

Magical Thinking

Like eyeblack before a game,
On goes the good-luck chapstick.

Fifteen push-ups on the floor,
Just to get the blood pumping.

Favorite shoes, the good belt,
Briefcase in the right hand.

Two blueberry muffins served
On the plate with the gold rim.

The lights all turn green on time,
Everything is right today.

Then – coffee catastrophe!
A spill on the lucky shirt.

Doomed.

Feel Like Gambling?

Game of chance! Blackjack, roulette, and craps, rolled into one.
Odds are, what you win or lose will have little

To do with what you put in, and while
Optimism's handy, it's luck you'll need when all 12 cards are

Jokers; the wheel's spinning; and the marbles keep flying off, lost.
Unless you strike a deal, and soon, you'll be
Rolling those dice and holding your breath, and
You know what they say about that. (Don't.)

The Courthouse

Many years ago they laid my bricks and mortar,
Noble in design, inspiring awe and wonder.
"The New County Courthouse" is what I'd be called,
Justice and truth would ring through my halls.

"If these walls could talk…" some buildings might say,
They've got nothing on what I observe here each day.
When I was first built, daily business was dignified,
If my founders could see me today, they'd be mortified.

Attorneys play dirty, stab each other in the backs,
Resorting all too often to personal attacks.
DAs hide the evidence, information gets leaked,
The only concern: an intact winning streak.

The call to the bench was once seen as respectable,
But now, it seems, any old clown is electable.
Judges and clerks are no strangers to cheating,
(They're banging more than gavels, if you catch my meaning.)

Not long ago all who walked through my door
Took care in selecting the outfits they wore.
Now flip-flops and T-shirts and low-riding jeans
Are giving me more of a view than I need.

Don't get me wrong now, I like local flavor.
A colorful character's something to savor.
But just a suggestion: For your date with the law,
Perhaps choose a shirt that covers your bra?

Grand settlements once took place on my steps,
Now my granite is covered in crushed cigarettes.
Where once my columns stood proud and pristine,
Graffiti now covers them – what does it mean?

Officials are saying I've gotten too small,
That my courtrooms and corridors can't handle it all.
Again and again, I've been shocked and amazed,
And I've come to agree: it's time to be razed.

Kenneth Branagh Prepares Evidence For Trial

To be or not to be; that is the question.
Whether 'tis nobler in my mind to affix
The stickers with numbers to my exhibits
Or to take the ones with letters and use those,
And by sticking them, alphabetize them all.
To choose; to label; no more. But I am stumped.
If I use numbers, what will people say?
That I think everything can be quantified?
That some exhibits are worth more than others?
That I am rating them somehow, 1 to 10?
But if it is to be letters instead, well...
Upper or lower case, then? Ay, there's the rub.
For of that choice, what perceptions might they have,
Those jurors, that judge, that courtroom, all looking,
All judging, all studying my decision.
Which stickers? Which stickers? It does give me pause,
Yet I must decide, so that I can move on.
Indeed: I shall go with the lettered stickers.
Numbers be damned, I am firm in this, my will,
And now shall stick them on to each exhibit:
A... B... C... Yes, this is looking excellent.
L...M...N....O...P...But soft! Where is the Q?
I must have lost it. My mistake, it pains me!
My failings are rendered here for all to see;
This flawed alphabet mocks my imperfection,
How I failed to control every detail.

Tales From The Table

See if you can follow these depositions…
The stories are doozies, weirder than fiction

"So, what did you do at work today?"
You May Wish You Hadn't Asked

Well, son, today I deposed an expert witness
In the field of organic farming
Who was called in to explain the ins and outs
Of manure use on crops – not such a simple issue, it seems,
Because you can't use raw manure on plants
Within a certain timeframe of harvest
If you want your crop to be certified organic,
Which was the very issue in question –
Whether indeed the "organic" products sold by the company
Had earned their name.
So you know what I looked at today?
Dated photos of manure.
Manure a month ago, manure a week ago, manure a day ago.
Oh, look! The manure piles are getting older.
They grow up so fast, don't they?
For four hours I did this.
Did I mention the guy's name was Rusty?
And that one document had "Rusty Manure Expert"
Written at the top?

When I Dreamed of Becoming an Attorney
I Wasn't Picturing Days Like This

Today I deposed a hooker,
Who blew the whistle, so to speak,
On her friend and... ah, business colleague
Who has been stealing from her clients,
Who, as it turns out, are very loyal customers
Because they are... well, they're addicted
To her – the hooker's friend who is also a hooker –
Because she has been... oh, how to put this...
She's been dusting her private parts with a new body powder
She made herself, which is
Not only lightly fragranced
But also made of about 20% cocaine.
It's a delicate process, you see,
Because you have to use some other ingredients in the powder
To keep it from getting... well, from getting too paste-like.
And you have to apply it just right.
She said,
"There's a lot of trial and error involved."

I'm Too Tired to Explain
What Happened to My Face

Today I was punched by an old man
Who believed I had been plotting against him for years
In cahoots with his ex-wife – or, to be clear,
His cat, to whom he was referring as his ex-wife
Throughout the 6-hour deposition,
In which he also explained that he was suffering
A variety of painful side effects
From the "surgical treatments"
Provided to him by the "doctor" being sued in this case
By hundreds of people
For implanting Jell-O – the food, like in hospitals – into people's bodies
Instead of legitimate breast implants.
The implants, you'll understand, were needed
By this 70-year-old man to complete his
Gender transformation,
As requested by his cat / ex-wife
Who it turns out is a lesbian.
Suggesting the implausibility of all this, was, apparently
Grounds for getting attacked across a table
By a supposedly "friendly witness,"
And that's how I'd explain this mark on my face if I were going to,
But I'm not.

I Wish I Could Un-See
The Things I Saw Today

Today I deposed a CEO
Of a tech company,
A guy no older than 50
Who can't possibly claim
Not to understand how the Internet works,
But who, still, used his work email address
To register for site after site
Filled with images of individuals
Who don't look like they're really enjoying
The things they're doing
With props such as spatulas and oven mitts.
And although the username on the accounts
("The Sperminator")
Looked an awful lot like the nickname on his embroidered golf towels
("The Hermanator")
He claimed to have no clue what we were showing him
Even as the blood drained
Right out of his face.

Life In the Firm

This is your tribe, from your bosses to your peers
The ones you'll love and hate for so many years

A Few More Haiku

Unprepared

No law class covered
"The Personal Problems of
Your Paralegal."

Reunion

"Remember that bitch
From first semester Contracts?"
"Yes, we've two kids now."

Modified Credo

Doing The Right Thing
(Or settling for doing
the least wrong of wrongs)

Saturday Night in December

There's no "holiday"
Or "party" about this crowd.
How long should we stay?

Cutbacks

Five lawyers let go.
Layoffs. (Not me.) My envy
Should tell me something.

Innovation

We're paperless now?
I just got comfortable
Using my voicemail.

Language Barrier

We use Latin terms
To make us feel smart and sharp
(Nobody else cares)

Misunderstood

We fight for justice,
Long nights, fluorescent lights. Still:
We're the butt of jokes.

The Upside to All This Computer Time

YouTube videos?
Funny emails? I see them
Before anyone.

Continuing Legal Education

The morning starts pleasantly enough,
Lukewarm coffee washes down stale raisin bagels,
Old friends and foes mill about, sharing war stories,
Then pick their seats, being careful not to get stuck near the front,
Or too far from the door closest to the restrooms.
A year has passed since the last CLE.
Complacency has seeped back in over time,
But everyone, including you, knows what is coming.

A program coordinator in a gray pantsuit, hair wound tightly in a bun,
Introduces the speaker without inflection or enthusiasm:
An expert with thirty years of experience
In whatever it is you practice.
On the foreheads of the assembled attendees,
Beads of sweat begin to form.

At first, a strange sense of confidence –
During the review of fundamental terms and concepts
You feel yourself nodding in agreement with the speaker,
Mumbling the answers to the simplest of questions
(Asked to no one in particular) under your breath.

Then you hear it. Like a bolt of lightning,
It rips through you.
Your heart races,
As you scribble in the margins of the manuscript,
The practice point you've been ignoring (unknowingly)
For your entire career.
The speaker's words run together into a dull hum,
As you scroll through your client list on the rolodex in your head,
Leaving mental asterisks next to the names of those who
Very well may come back to sue you.

The panic continues to strike in bursts,
Until, like a fighter in a late round,
You no longer feel the sting of the punches.
Finally, a break is called.

Hanging your head low, you fix your gaze upon
The institutional pattern of the carpet floor
And follow it to the refreshments table in the back of the room.
As you reach for a generic chocolate chip cookie,
You notice your hand is shaking ever so slightly.

Soon it will begin again.

Ode to the Rainmaker

With thanks for the inspiration to Elizabeth Barrett Browning

How do I love thee? Let me count the ways.
You reek of charm, the genetically blessed,
And while I spend my hours in this office,
You're on some golf course or other most days.
Your intellect is at best rather base,
Your work product is far below the rest,
Your attitude is I-couldn't-care-less,
When I clean up your mess, you get the praise.
Family connections and a silver spoon,
Like a nephew in the mob you're plugged in.
What's to love, then? It's simple. Selfish, too:
I like having a job, money to spend.
And as little true law work as you do,
You've the golden touch at bringing it in.

Reconnaissance

I just wanted a peek at the guy, but
Guess what? Turns out
Scoping out opposing counsel online
Hurts more than it helps.

Guess what? Turns out
Even at our age (same graduating year!)
He wears slim-cut shirts
And has all his hair – the kind women are always touching.

Scoping out opposing counsel online
Also produces a four-page list of victories,
Not to mention pro bono service awards
(And here I thought Jesus was a carpenter.)

Hurts more than it helps,
Frankly, to realize I may have published an article
On this very type of case,
But he wrote a book… which I just ordered.
(Free shipping! Who's winning now?)

Thoughts From a Heavy Book

There was a time when we books reigned supreme,
Bound paper treasures held in high esteem.
We'd spend days spread out on office tables,
Pored over and marked with sticky labels.
But once lawyers started using laptops,
We have become nothing more than mere props.
I hear them say that we're now obsolete,
That we're taking up room and can't compete.
We do not deserve this kind of abuse!
Surely someone can put us to good use?
Wait. I think I see the maintenance man.
He's got a large container. What's his plan?
Is this the answer to my many prayers?
Someone still needs us? Someone really cares?
The box on both sides reads "Recycle Bin."
What's that? Is it good? Let the fun begin!

Pro Boner

I was trying to find some purpose,
Something to fill my soul,
I needed to grasp onto some meaning,
To make myself feel whole.

"Do some pro bono," someone told me,
"Help out your fellow man."
I thought: "Of course, that's the spirit!"
I set out, full of pep, on a plan.

I approached our managing partner,
And made my intentions known.
He nodded, said, "I've got just the thing,"
With a smirk behind his tone.

What honorable service awaited?
Helping the old or the poor?
Advising a righteous nonprofit?
My excitement grew even more.

And that's when I learned the specifics,
The story of a local inmate
Caught fondling his privates repeatedly
By a prison guard who grew irate.

The prisoner was forced to wear red,
So everyone else would see
He couldn't keep his hands off himself –
A mark of shame for the detainee.

And so it seemed I'd fill my void,
Making this humiliation cease,
My noble charge: to see that this man
Could masturbate in peace.

The Editor

How I rue the invention of "track changes"
In Microsoft Word
And your compulsion to use it
Every
Freaking
Time
A document passes in front of your eyes.

Could you at least use a font color
Other than red
When you delete whole paragraphs?
Complaints,
Motions,
Contracts
Are bleeding to death on my screen.

Also: A brief is not a yes-or-no question
Or even a question at all,
So when you write only NO on my draft
(What
the
hell?)
I'm not sure which part you're referring to.

Furthermore, does it really matter
How I sign letters?
When you cross out "Sincerely" in favor of
"Yours
Very
Truly"
I don't see what difference it makes.

And while I am sorry I used "therefore" once
Instead of "heretofore,"
And I know it was wrong, you can stop putting
"Are
you
sure?"
Next to either word every time I use it.

Furthermore, your psychotic devotion to placing
Two spaces after every period
Is slowly but effectively driving me mad, because
THAT'S
FOR
TYPEWRITERS
IN 1970, DAMMIT.

Saturdays

With recognition of Phillip Lopate's "We Who Are Your
Closest Friends" for inspiration

We who are
your senior partners
in the firm
think the time is right
to tell you
that we have been meeting
on the golf course every Saturday,
plotting and planning
ways to keep you feeling
discouraged
discomfited
disappointed
and in a state of
constant paranoia,
by neither praising you
for a job well done,
nor firing you for complete
incompetence.
Your fellow associates are
in on it,
as is your assistant,
and the guy who changes
the toner in your printer;
and we have agreed to
keep you unbalanced:
just enough to undermine your confidence,
but not enough to make you snap.
We realize that by telling you this,
we risk providing you with
the very stability you crave,
some modicum of calm

as you bob and thrash
in this tumultuous sea.
But ever since our Saturdays on the course
have brought us
a collective purpose,
with you as the center of attention,
we have refrained
from biting off
each other's heads
and stabbing each other
in the backs.
So we were kind of hoping
you might continue to
flounder about
in search of approval,
if not as a natural result
of your position,
then for the good of firm morale.

The Shark

Compromise, kindness – no, that's not my story.
Cold and brutal is how I leave my mark.
Am I bloodthirsty? Yes, law can get gory.
Killer instincts earned my nickname: The Shark.

Work always comes first, that's a motto of mine,
And decisions are based on the dollar.
Don't bother me with your personal life –
I've no time for those who are smaller.

As much as I'd lived and worked true to shark form,
Wielding power by inspiring fright,
I was shocked one morning to find that I'd morphed
Into the real thing overnight.

I struggled, at first, with this change so bizarre,
My razor-sharp scales ripped my suits,
And I couldn't quite drive my beloved sports car
With fins that wouldn't fit into shoes.

But strangely, people were unfazed by me,
As though they had long been expecting this,
They still showed me the same fear – respect, I mean –
Could it be that they just didn't notice?

The firm members treated me just like always,
No one noted my new row of teeth.
The associates I approached averted their gaze,
The way they usually do when we meet.

I thought for sure they would have seen the way,
When I lunched on my raw tuna steak,
My eyes rolled back while attacking my prey,
And my bite made the china plate break.

Later my ex-wife made not one remark,
When I saw her outside with our son.
He shook my side fin, standing there in the park,
Not surprised at what I'd become.

Do I ever remember, think back to before
And the feel of my once-human skin?
No. Sharks don't go backward — they only move forth —
And a shark is what I've always been.

Sisterhood

It's dawning on me now that we are not
Thelma and Louise, Laverne and Shirley,
Cagney and Lacey, or Oprah and Gayle,
We don't sing *R-E-S-P-E-C-T,*
Or *Sisters Are Doing It For Themselves,*
Or even *I Am Woman, Hear Me Roar,*
We don't "stick it to the man" together,
Or hammer away at the glass ceiling,
Or break down the walls of the old boys club,
Because there is no solidarity,
No sacred girl code or "hos before bros."
We're the only two females on this team,
And in front of everyone it was you
Who sent me out of the room for coffee.

Just Kidding

Once upon a time there was a pyramid,
A solid structure nobody could budge.
At the top there sat a pack of partners,
Taking turns performing tricks before the judge.
At the bottom, hungry law grads throwing elbows,
And jostling for the greatest share of crumbs,
All stepping on each other's toes and fingers,
Just to climb a little closer to the sun.

If we took a break from all this sweaty striving,
And quit counting up the hours like they're bricks,
We'd have to laugh, right? After all, it's nonsense
To slave away so greedily like this.
What if we ditched this model, started fresh?
Yes! Screw this madness! Now our time is due!
Let's walk away and put it all behind us…
I'll stop climbing just as soon as you do.

The Barrister's Ball

I've been around for a while now.
I thought I'd seen it all,
But that was before I attended
My first Barrister's Ball.

One night each year it happens,
When all the true Type-A's
Cast off their shells and suit jackets,
Inhibitions put away.

The alcohol flows freely,
The band strikes up a tune,
Lawyers transform before your eyes,
Like beasts under a full moon.

You know that bankruptcy expert,
The uptight one from the third floor?
She climbed onstage and rapped *Gold Digger.*
(I didn't know she swore.)

The managing partner danced himself
Right into the cocktail shrimp.
Tiny silver forks went flying.
Tomorrow he'll have a limp.

One of the summer associates,
Who hit the Johnnie Black,
Made a pass at a partner's wife.
He can't take that one back.

The quiet guy from across the hall
Was talking too close to my face
And grabbing the ass of each woman he passed
Under the guise of a friendly embrace.

A disheveled litigator sat slumped,
Crying to another…
Something about his wasted dreams
And letting down his mother.

Two family law practitioners
Stole a bottle from the bar,
And took shots from votive candle holders
On the hood of someone's car.

Two more got into an argument,
One claimed the other had lied,
About what, I'm not sure. But one slapped the other,
And then they hugged and cried.

Three women danced to *Twist and Shout*
And caused quite an uproar,
When they twisted down but couldn't get up
And fell into a heap on the floor.

A former judge passed out in the stairwell
His tuxedo all rumpled and drenched.
When I tried to rouse him, he called me Maria
And cursed me in Spanish and French.

On Monday, we all avoid eye contact,
While the rumors and whispers abound,
But by Tuesday it's back to business as usual,
Until next year's Ball comes around.

Vacation

first night at the beach.
surf sounds and a cool, cleansing breeze
have brought forgiveness from loved ones
for not leaving the office sooner this morning.
innumerable stars give the appearance of a vast,
distant city in the otherwise black sky.
ghost crabs peek out from their holes in the sand near where I stand,
breathing.

[BUZZ]

a sudden, invasive brightness frightens them back underground.

[BUZZ]

the harsh light spreads into the night air.
stars fade.

no. not [BUZZ] now.

it's no use to hope for spam.
the office center by the check-in desk in the lobby awaits,
tinted glass allowing in
judgmental stares from disbelieving vacationers.

three days have passed.
one meal and a half with my family and a short trip to the alligator farm
and that's it,
but it could have been worse.
all is not lost.
one day remains.
but first, sleep – it is late.

the waves pound and recede.
the sheets – have they been this soft all week? – fold closed around me.
sleep
             pulls
                        me
                                  under.

[BUZZ]

a blue glow fills the room.

Passive Aggression In Writing

To: Lessee's Attorney <Jim>
From: Lessor's Attorney <Barb>

> *Jim, please see attached draft of the lease agreement. Note that my client is requiring that the lessee maintain at least $1M in general liability insurance. -Barb*

CC: Barb's Partner

> *Barb, I don't see an attachment, but my client is not going to agree to $1.5M. -Jim*

CC: Barb's Partner, Jim's Partner

> *Thanks for your thoughtful note, Jim. It's $1M, as you'll see in the insurance provision, which was part of the lease attached in the original email. You have to click on the paperclip icon. -Barb*

CC: Barb's Partner, Jim's Partner, Barb's Assistant Megan

> *Barb, I'm ready to review the document, but you seem unable to attach it.*
>
> *Megan, please fax me the lease Barb is referring to. -Jim*

CC: Barb's Partner, Jim's Partner, Barb's Assistant Megan,
Jim's Client

*Megan, there's no need to fax anything. Jim, I'm sorry you're
unable to operate email.*

*Since you seem to be having technical issues, I'm copying
your client on this directly. If you two could please take a
look at the lease agreement and get back to me, that would be
great. -Barb*

CC: Barb's Partner, Jim's Partner, Barb's Assistant Megan, Jim's
Client, Barb's Client; Barb's Paralegal; Another of Barb's Partners

*Barb, when you're ready to get me the lease agreement, I will
review it. Until that time, I will ask that you not contact my
client and also that you take note of my prior statement that
my client will not entertain the figure of $1.5M in liability
insurance.*

To: Jim's client
From: Barb's client

Let's just meet for lunch today and work this out ourselves.

A Way With Words

"May it please the court," she began,
Before asking Your Honor's permission
To approach the bench and confer
On a point that needed clarity.

"A moment, please?" she asked,
When lowering her voice and discussing
A matter discreetly with her client,
Head bowed to convey respect.

"No further questions at this time," she said,
After she'd posed her last inquiry
With elocution so flawless as to be sure
The record would reflect each word.

"Dear Sir," began the document
She drafted that afternoon, replete
With punctuation, indentation, and italics,
Not to mention a flourish of Latin.

"What a $#% mother#@* bunch of @#$!"
She hollered at happy hour, snorting with laughter,
Swapping stories with colleagues in language
That made the bartender, a former Marine, blush.

To Generation Y, From Your Partners

I'm not really sure how you made it this far,
With grammar so bad, social skills so bizarre.
Since you're able to connect only in shorthand,
Let me put this in terms that you can understand:

u r driving me mad w/ ur emails like txts,
when I read them I am left completely perplexed,
so next time, use real words like "whereupon"
and remember, I don't speak emoticon.

and 1 more thing u do that I cannot condone,
when I'm talking to u, stop looking at ur phone!
I know, I know… u may call me a hater
but pls learn 2 communicate, k? C U L8R.

The Bulldog

Unscrupulous? Sleazy?
Yes. Machiavellian? Conscienceless? These also would work.
He prefers "The Bulldog."

Who picks his own nickname?
This guy. For "tenacity." Believes in action. Courtesy and
Ethics are optional.

Discovery requests?
A game. Wear everyone down with minutiae. Claim privilege.
Ask for it all. Give naught.

Settlement? Forget it.
He threatens sanctions for bringing frivolous and deceptive
Claims (all unwarranted).

Have something that he needs?
He'll get it. Pay a maid, hijack a delivery. Cross that
Imaginary line.

And when I'm in trouble?
Don't think I won't remember his slick maneuvers, shady deals.
He's the first one I'll call.

Disillusionment: The Limericks

There may be some contrast, in moments of doubt,
Between what you hoped for and how things turned out

Big Law Associate, Year One

Last summer it seemed so sincere,
Luxe parties, boondoggles, good cheer,
But now that's all done,
And there's no time for fun,
When I'm billing three thousand a year.

"Friends"

When you see me around and about,
I'm so pleased when you give me a shout,
But my mood will turn bleak,
If free counsel you seek.
Ask how I'm doing, not for a handout.

Role Model

My mentor seemed nothing but good,
I followed him best as I could,
But I became scarred,
When he got disbarred,
Seems all I believed was falsehood.

Partnership Traaaaaaaaaaaaaaaaack

I was promised the partnership track,
I've stayed loyal and on the right tack,
But the partners keep meeting,
Despite all my pleading,
And moving the finish line back.

Job Security

When the crash came and my job was through,
I was unsure just what I would do,
This wasn't the math
I banked on with this path,
Now I pay the bills with doc review.

Riches to Rags

My just-fine career plan I ditched
For law school so I could get rich,
Now there's not one job prospect
And I'm burdened with debt
And I wish I could un-make the switch.

Government Lawyer

While my friends at big firms get abused,
I'm relaxed and quite often amused.
Though my suits may be shabby,
At least I'm not crabby.
(Could you spot me some cash for bar dues?)

Lofty Notions

Like Atticus Finch I'd defend
Good people right up to the end,
But they're not always kind,
And I've since come to find,
Tom Robinson was just pretend.

Going In-House

I left my big law firm with glee,
But there's one thing I didn't foresee:
Though the clients I'd had
Might have driven me mad,
They were better than corporate VPs.

Closing Argument

Even the best job comes with a few glitches
And some less-than-desirable aspects,
And every workplace has its sons-of-bitches
Mixed in with those deserving of respect.

Some days you're on fire, you're a superhero,
Winning cases and clients left and right.
Other days rank at somewhere below zero,
Seems like everyone's spoiling for a fight.

You could cope with the rough days by freaking out,
You could slam the phone, knock over your plant,
You could stomp around, kick the wall, curse out loud,
Or type it out in an ill-advised rant.

But what's the point in becoming frustrated,
In getting your knickers into a twist?
Aren't times like these why humor was created,
The very reason why laughter exists?

No one knows the law like us lawyers, indeed,
And no one else gets all the inside jokes.
So when the job feels like it's making you bleed,
Look around: you've got friends in these folks.

To this esteemed club, each of you a member,
We hope you enjoyed reading this verse.
(And if it helps you, then always remember:
Doctors probably have it much worse.)

Acknowledgments

We are so grateful to those who helped this book see the light of day, namely –

A group of attorneys and editors who took the time to read every single poem and offer feedback: John DuPuy, Andy Johnson, Jeff Kent, Tina Hsu, Missy Owen, Brittany Roberts, and Tony Tuntasit.

The Dead Mule School of Southern Literature, which published "Sisterhood" before we even had the book finished.

More friends than we could possibly list here (but hope to thank in person), who provided advice and offered support of all kinds.

JD's law partners, whose utmost professionalism and persistent kindness forced him to search for inspiration in far away places for the more inauspicious characters portrayed in this book.

And especially Cherie, John, and our families, for their patience.

About the Authors

JD DuPuy is a practicing attorney in Charlotte, North Carolina.

ML Philpott is a freelance writer in Atlanta, Georgia.

They have been friends since their days at Davidson College.

38592692R00057

Made in the USA
Middletown, DE
20 December 2016